KILLING THE

MULLINS

AND THE AFTERMATH

BY OAKLEY DEAN BALDWIN

Copyright © 2015 ODB Publishing

Check out my other stories and books at:

http://thebaldwinstories.wix.com/author-blog

In loving memory of my mother, Lora Ellen Beverly Baldwin, born September 5, 1935, to Oakley Rufus Beverly and Beulah Mae Mullins in Letcher, Kentucky.

PROLOGUE

This work is based mostly on family history, folklore, historical facts, court documents, tombstones, and newspaper articles that were available at the time of writing.

Information was gathered from multiple sources and pieced together into a historical fiction story. As such, it should not be a definite source of information. Of course, after more than one hundred and twenty years, stories are told and retold, with facts becoming harder to find. I am listing this story as fiction based on a true family story.

This story explores my mother's first cousin three times removed, Ira "Bad Ira" Mullins. This story was handed down to my mother who enlightened me, as I have done with my children. My mother would passionately share this story when I was a young boy. She wrote many other stories and poems that I plan to share with you all at a later date.

This story is one of the wildest stories ever told to me as well as one of my absolute favorites. I hope you are entertained as much as I have been over the years.

The Mullins families were early settlers to Letcher County, Kentucky, Wise County, Virginia, and parts of southern West Virginia.

A cousin of Ira Mullins named Andrew Jackson Mullins founded the town of Mullens in Wyoming County, West Virginia in 1894. The town's original name Mullins, was spelled with an "i"; but a failure to dot the "i" in Mullins led to the name being misread by the Legislature as Mullens and recorded this way.

On February 7, 1894, Andrew Jackson Mullins purchased a tract of 69 acres at the mouth of Slab Fork, West Virginia. He cleared the land for farm use and then built a log home for his family. In 1897, Mullins built a log cabin to serve as a schoolhouse and a church.

Andrew Jackson Mullins would continue to serve the town he created for many years.

Andrew served two terms as Justice of the Peace, two terms as Mayor, and was twice elected to the House of Delegates. On February 26, 1938, Andrew Jackson Mullins passed away at age eight one and was buried in Flat Top, West Virginia, to where he still lies today.

I was completely unaware of this family connection and history when I lived in the Town of Mullens and was stationed in Wyoming County as a West Virginia State Trooper in the late 1970's.

Ironically, Ephraim "Eph-of-All" Hatfield was the great grandfather of Andrew Jackson Mullins as well as the great grandfather of William Anse "Devil Anse" Hatfield the famous patriarch of the well-known feud between the Hatfield and McCoy families.

TABLE OF CONTENTS

Part One
A Tale to Tell

We will never know the real complete story with the feud between Ira "Bad Ira" Mullins and Doc Marshall Benton "Red Fox" Taylor (or referred to simply as Doc Taylor from here forward) which led to the death of both men. This feud reached a climax with the killing known as "The Pound Gap Massacre" at the natural pass road in the Appalachian and Pine Mountain range at the state border of Wise County Virginia and Letcher County Kentucky. This same road was used by Daniel Boone in 1774 to warn land surveyors of a possible attack from the local Shawnee Indians. Boone referred to the Pound Gap as the "Sounding Gap".

We do know Ira Mullins was known as a corn whisky runner, a moonshiner and a small time merchant. His unfortunate turn of events started once his family settled on land near Jenkins, Kentucky owned by Henry Vanover.

Over 900 acres of land was deeded to Henry Vanover by the Federal government for his services in the Union Army during the Civil War. Henry married Sarah Jane Bentley and they had many children.

Ira Mullins was born in Kentucky on February 8, 1857, to John L. Mullins and Martha A. Potter. The parents of John L. Mullins were Sherwood Mullins and Mary Ann Roberts.

Ira's father was a merchant and a shoemaker. Ira's hard life started as a young boy. Ira was about thirteen years old when his father was found murdered in the woods not far from their home. His father John L. Mullins was about forty two years old at the time of his unfortunate demise.

I can't imagine the devastation of not only losing your father but having to become a man at such a formative stage in life. This must have been at times overwhelming for Ira to have to deal with. One day Ira was a young teen and the next day he was the man of the house.

What a burden to place on a young man. It must have seemed like he was carrying the weight of the world on his shoulders.

He was now the provider for his mother and siblings as well as himself.

Ira was twenty two years old when he married Louranza Estep on May 10, 1879. Louranza was born 1859 in Kentucky to Anderson J. Estep and Mary Rebecca Vanover. Mary was the sister of property owner Henry Vanover. Ira and Louranza apparently took up homesteading on Louranza's uncle Henry Vanover's family property.

Up until the time of the Civil War, moonshine was not regulated and it was legal to make. With the arrival of the war, the government started taxing moonshine to help fund military expenses. Times were hard for mountain folks back then and the extra income made on moonshine helped in making ends meet.

Henry Vanover was in the timber business and apparently did not care for moonshine operations on his property.

Knowing that Ira was a moonshiner, Henry attempted to have Ira Mullins removed from his property which caused hard feelings and problems between the two men.

I feel certain that all of this caused family problems and drama amongst the rest of the family members also. Louranza's mother was Henry's sister and their mother must have spent a lot of time worrying over this situation.

No doubt since Ira was married to Henry Vanover's niece, Ira took high offence to being forced off of family property.

The story was told that Ira Mullins was so upset that he hired an assassin to kill his wife's uncle Henry Vanover.

In March 1885, one day while Henry was relaxing, eating dinner with his wife and children at his home, a man named James Roberts from Ohio who had been staying over at Ira Mullin's home came from the woods riding a horse firing his rifle at Henry Vanover narrowly missing him.

In defense, Henry got his rifle and returned fire killing James Roberts. Henry Vanover was tried for killing James Roberts but was acquitted on June 18, 1887.

The Courier-Journal of Louisville Kentucky reported on July 25, 1885:

"Cases before Judge Jackson: The case Judge Jackson was appointed to try are Henry Vanover, for the shooting of James Roberts; Samuel, William and Martine Holcomb, for killing Samuel Cornet, and Wash Craft, for killing Cook and Wiley Craft. In the first of these opinion is somewhat divided. Vanover's friends claim the following to be the state of facts.

One morning last March, Roberts passed Vanover's house, and, stopping in front, fired three shots through the trees in the direction of the dwelling.

Vanover and a large family were eating in front on the porch, but, fortunately, escaped. Vanover then got down his Winchester, waited on the hillside till Roberts return, and dropped him.

Witnesses for the prosecution scout the idea that such is the true state of affairs, but it is the straightest account your correspondent has been able to gather. Vanover is out on bond."

Unfortunately for Henry, not too long after he was acquitted from this shooting, the grim reaper caught up with him.

On June 28, 1887, Henry was hoeing crops in his fields with his wife Sarah when he was ambushed from the woods and killed by an unknown assassin. Word got out that Clifton Branham came into some money but no one reportedly knew exactly where it came from, and if they did know they weren't telling it. Clifton Branham and his brother Tandy were arrested and tried for the murder of Henry. During the trial Clifton Branham claimed, "I got some money for the killing, but I did not kill Henry Vanover."They were both convicted and spent several years in prison.

The rumor was that Ira Mullins or Devil John Wright, another local outlaw was behind the killing and had paid Clifton and Tandy Branham to kill Henry Vanover. Yet, Ira was never linked to the killing. Many people believed Devil John Wright may have been behind it since he received some of Henry Vanover's land through court claims directly after the killing.

During this same time, Henry's daughter Catherine was dating a man named Samuel McHenan (Henan) Fleming (or referred to simply as Henan Fleming from here forward) and his brother Preston McCalvin (Calvin) Fleming (or referred to simply as Calvin Fleming from here forward) were visitors at the Vanover house on many occasions, they were both very good friends with a man named Doc Taylor.

The parents of Henan and Calvin Fleming were Robert Jefferson Fleming and Margaret Rose. Margaret Rose's parents were Samuel Rose and Margaret Cantrell.

Catherine Vanover married Henan Fleming in September of 1887and moved to Washington State. Catherine and Henan stayed in Washington State for some time, and then moved back to handle some of the property issues from her father's estate due to the court claims of Devil John Wright.

Doc Taylor was born on May 8, 1836 in Taylorstown, Scott County, Virginia to William P. Taylor and Mary Stallard. Doc married Nancy Ann Booth.

However, the family of his next arrangement with a significant other would help lead him to the gallows and the hangman's noose.

Doc was raised on a farm and came from a very honorable family. He was a herb doctor and studied under his uncle Dr. Morgan L. Stallard of Lee County, Virginia. In 1861, Doc was called into the military with the Confederate States of America (CSA) and served with the 64th Virginia Calvary. Some say he deserted shortly after the war started and hid out in the mountains until after the war. Others say he was a hero in the war.

Doc continued practicing medicine and even started preaching. For over ten years, he lived a mostly uneventful and quiet life.

In 1876, after years of practicing medicine and hard work, he was accused of killing Robert Moore a local outlaw and moonshiner of western Virginia. The story goes like this...One night, late at night while resting with his wife at his home, Robert Moore was shot and killed. Several of Robert's neighbors were convinced that Doc Taylor had murdered him.

Taylor was arrested for the murder, but after a trial by jury he was acquitted, mainly because no witnesses would testify against him.

With his military service in the Civil War, he was not bashful about speaking his mind. As a preacher, Doc had a dislike for moonshiners and outlaws. He even accepted a Deputy Marshall position in Wise County, Virginia to combat the spreading growth of illegal moonshining.

Doc Taylor's life took another turn in the late 1880's. His arrangement with his significant other was to a cousin of Ira Mullins; her name was Rebecca Jane Mullins. She was born in May 1855 in Wise County, Virginia. Rebecca was first married to Jeremiah M. Bolling who was a direct descendent of Colonel Robert Bolling and Jane Rolfe. Jane Rolfe was the granddaughter of Pocahontas. Rebecca's parents were Booker Basil "Cripple Basil" Mullins and America Baker; America Baker's parents were Richard Baker and Abigail Beverly.

The Children of Doc Taylor and Rebecca Jane Mullins were: America Mullins (she married Marshall Mullins), Charlie Todd Mullins Taylor, and James Calvin Mullins Taylor (who married Delphia Mullins).

The first known encounter between Ira "Bad Ira" Mullins and Doc Taylor happened as Ira Mullins was riding in a wagon hauling a load of moonshine through the Wise Courthouse community.

Doc Taylor had gathered a posse of men and captured the wagon with its load. Over 250 shots were fired between the two groups during this encounter, many were wounded, and the driver of the Mullins wagon was killed. Ira Mullins and several others got away but it is thought that Ira Mullins was one of the wounded and was partially paralyzed from his wounds.

Due to the time it would take to gather together a posse of men one could only wonder if one of Rebecca Jane Mullins's extended family members warned Doc Taylor that Ira Mullins was coming with a wagon load of moonshine.

After this reckless and careless shootout endangering other local citizens, Doc Taylor was himself becoming an oddity. He almost always dressed in black clothing and his horse was a large black fox trotter. He carried several weapons with him at all times, a Colt 45 caliber pistol on both sides, two ammo belts across his chest, a long Winchester rifle and a five foot long brass-tipped spyglass. Some folks became afraid of his reckless behavior and he soon was released from his duties as Deputy Marshall.

Over the next several months, tensions escalated with both men issuing threats and calling each other out. This escalated to the point that Doc Taylor feared for his own life. One night he was accused of firing a shot at Ira Mullins through Ira's bedroom window while Ira was in bed. The shot was so close it actually caught the bed on fire but missed Ira Mullins.

Ira Mullins accused Doc Taylor of trying to kill him. Consequently, the rumor commenced that Ira Mullins could not protect himself (being paralyzed) and thus placed a $300 bounty on Doc Taylor's head.

One must understand that the value of $300 in the 1890's is equivalent to almost $8000 now in today's money.

Doc Taylor traveled the countryside telling folks he encountered in the area that Ira Mullins had indeed put a bounty out on his head and was trying to have him killed.

Doc Taylor was questioned by law enforcement officials about the shooting and had an alibi. He claimed he was staying with a family in Kentucky for a period of time delivering a baby when the shot was fired into Ira Mullins' bed.

PART TWO
THE MULLIN'S MASSACRE

On May 14, 1892, the feud escalated into a bloody massacre. Evidence that was discovered (including cut and dried branches left between large rocks at the crime scene) pointed to the massacre being contrived with premeditated efforts. Sometime (maybe the day before) three or four men waited for Ira Mullins and his family to reach the Pound Gap or what is now known as the Killing Rock.

Again, how were the travel plans of Ira Mullins revealed to Doc Taylor who waited for him on the Pound Gap road? Doc would have had to have been tipped off a day or two in advance to give him the necessary time to plot his attack with his henchmen. These perpetrators undoubtedly would have needed specific information to be able to successfully lay in wait at the exact time and place.

In the mountains of Kentucky, early May is a good time to start moonshining as the leaves on the trees start to grow and provide ample cover for brewing illegal alcohol. Also, in order to stay out of sight of the Law, moonshiners normally conducted their operations deep in the woods at night under the moon light. There was several ways back then to make moonshine; many used malted barley, cracked corn, sugar, distillers yeast, and water as the main ingredients. A steady stream of cold water and dry wood for fuel for the fire was also important.

It would have taken Ira Mullins several days of back breaking work to make enough moonshine to fill several large barrels to make up a wagon load.

Somehow, Doc Taylor was advised that Ira Mullins completed a brew of moonshine and would be headed from Kentucky to Virginia following the Pound Gap road.

Did Doc Taylor have spies or could this information have spread from kinfolk carelessly gossiping about Ira Mullins traveling up to Pound Gap that day?

This show down would be the second one in less than two years between the two men since Doc Taylor and Rebecca Jane Mullins had become a couple.

Calvin and Henan Fleming were apparently enlisted by Doc Taylor and had some motivation to assist anyway. Henan Fleming had his own suspicions that Ira Mullins was involved with the killing of his father-in-law (Henry Vanover) about five years earlier. Thus, he still had strong contempt for Ira Mullins.

It was also believed that Henry Adams of Kentucky may have been involved as the fourth assassin; Henry was indicted but was never brought to trial. Rumor had it that his rifle was used by one of the killers even though he was never placed at the scene of the crime by any witnesses.

The assassins lie in wait for the Mullins family party behind the brush and several large rocks until about mid-day on May 14, 1892.

That morning, the Mullins family all left Wilson Mullins home near Cane Creek Branch on Kentucky Pine Mountain and headed for Virginia's Old Fincastle Trail.

The travel party consisted of the following people: Ira Mullins, his wife Louranza, their fourteen year old son John Harrison Mullins, Ira's sister Amanda Jane Mullins, her husband Wilson Mullins, and two hired hands fifteen year old Greenberry Harris and John Chappel.

Wilson Mullins was at the point walking in front of the wagon, John Chappel was holding the reins driving the wagon load of moonshine and Louranza was sitting on the bench seat beside John. Since Ira was already partially paralyzed from a previous shooting, he was propped up lying in the back of the wagon high upon the straw covering the moonshine barrels. Amanda Jane was riding a horse alongside of the wagon. Greenberry Harris and John Harrison Mullins were walking not very far behind the wagon.

The five foot brass-tipped spy glass that Doc Taylor used would give the assassins plenty of notice when the Mullins party was approaching.

The smell and sounds of the forest, with the birds chirping, the wagon creaking along, the young boys throwing stones at different trees and talking about young boy things, mostly nothing, were all part of a peaceful, routine trip. The party was totally unaware of the calamities that lie ahead.

The Mullins party rolled on like lambs to the slaughter. The wagon just had reached Pound Gap and it was then that the sounds of the first shots ended the all too quiet journey. The tranquil setting on the rocky trail suddenly transformed into unfathomable bloodshed, disbelief, horror, and sorrow.

Numerous masked men began discharging their rifles twenty to thirty feet away from the right side of the trail as well as above the dirt road. This was a complete act of madness and cowardice aimed at the Mullins party.

More than likely the Mullins party would have been carrying a weapon or two with them, but there was no evidence that any of the Mullins party returned fire at the killers.

A pull horse fell dead almost immediately from the gunfire; John Harrison Mullins indicated he witnessed this along with Wilson Mullins being shot and staggering. In horror and fear John started running in the opposite direction (back toward Kentucky) and ran as hard as he possibly could. Fortunately, even though the bullets struck his clothing, his body was unharmed.

He heard numerous shots during his roughly half mile run and he then finally stopped to look back. Needless to say, his heart had been nearly pounding out of his chest.

The Pound Gap air was thick with the sight and smell of black powder. Now it is strongly believed that the murderers cruelly shot the pull horses to lessen the chances that the Mullins party could escape their wrath.

Ira Mullins was the victim of eight gunshot wounds. The killers likely shot him in the head at close range toward the end of the massacre ensuring he was finished off for good.

Louranza Mullins was struck by a bullet while sitting on the wagon bench. Still, she was able to move down the wagon behind the wheel and shouted for Amanda Jane Mullins to come to her.

Amanda Jane left her horse and sprinted to her husband and found he was shot, she then ran to Louranza pulling her sister-in-law up into a sitting position. Louranza looked at Amanda Jane and uttered, "They have killed me."

Once the gun firing ceased and the smoke cleared, Amanda Jane saw three men standing behind the rocks, which from this time on has become known as the "Killing Rock". These men had green veils that partially covered the upper part of their faces.

Amanda Jane screamed at the men, "Boys, for the Lord's sake, don't shoot anymore; you have killed them all now. Let me stay with them till someone finds us."

Each of the henchmen shouted threats and cursed at Amanda Jane. The voice of Calvin Fleming stood out to her as well as the possible voice of the notorious Doc Taylor.

At this time, one of the killers asked the others to spare the life of Amanda Jane; she recognized this voice most likely as that of Henan Fleming. Then, one of the shooters yelled, "G—D--- you, take to the road and leave or we will kill you too."

Still fearing for her life, Amanda Jane using every drop of adrenalin coursing through her veins fled knowing her very life depended on it; she took full advantage of the opportunity given to her and ran for her life down the dirt road toward Virginia. Her horse had headed in the same direction, once mounted on her horse; the killers took aim and started firing at her.

Thankfully, she was not harmed and managed to ride her horse roughly eighteen miles into the community of Jenkins near the Elkhorn River.

Louranza Mullins sustained gunshot wounds to both her breasts and knees. The killers took her handbag from her belt and one that was tied to the wagon and flipped her apron up and over her head.

Supposedly between $400 and $1,000 was taken from her handbag alone. However, revenge and sheer hatred were the ultimate reasons for these murders and the act of robbery was a mere bonus.

As for John Chappel, he was shot six times. Greenberry Harris was shot in the head as well as the heart and Wilson Mullins suffered a fatal chest wound. John Harrison Mullins was able to escape to the home of George Francisco and reported the horrible crime. From there, the news rapidly spread and many men angrily stormed off to the Pound Gap with their guns searching for the killers.

In the aftermath of the slaughter the killers had fled, with Amanda and John having escaped. The rest of the Mullins party lied dead on the Pound Gap trail, no sounds of wild life, no breeze, everything being calm and quiet except for the sound of the blood seeping into the ground. Reminding me of the story in the Bible of where Cain slew Abel and God said, what hast thou done? The voice of thy brother's blood crieth unto me from the ground.

A crew of twenty men was quickly assembled and they gathered the 45.75 caliber spent shell casings from the rifles and pistols shell casings while investigating the crime scene. They began hunting for the killers but sadly the trail had become cold. It appeared the killers had escaped into the rugged mountain side.

The Mullins friends and family members recovered the bodies and made the proper funeral preparations. The deceased individuals were taken back to Wilson Mullins' home.

Several of the deceased had to be placed on the front porch as the home simply did not have the space to accommodate them all inside. A large fire had to be started near the porch to help keep the flies away from the decomposing bodies.

William Potter, Ira Mullins's brother in Law, allowed all the members to be buried in the nearby Potter family Cemetery. Their family placed the following words on Ira and Louanza's head stone:

Tis hard to break the tender cord,

When love had bound the heart.

Tis hard so hard to speak the works "We must forever part"

Dearest loved ones we have laid thee in thy peaceful grave's embrace.

But thy memory will be cherished Till we see thy heavenly face.

It turns out the inscription that was placed by family loved ones on the tombstone "Dearest loved ones we have laid thee in the peaceful graves." was short lived.

Just four months after Ira and his family were murdered, Ira's grave was desecrated. Someone blew up his grave with dynamite exposing his remains.

The Richmond Dispatch described the incident as follows:

IRA MULLINS GRAVE DESECRATED Ghouls Dynamite the Remains [correspondence of the Richmond Dispatch]

"Clintwood, VA., August 15 - The grave of Ira Mullins, the man who was murdered near Pound Gap last spring, has lately been desecrated in an inhumane manner. Some ghoulish wretches blew the grave up with dynamite or some other explosive substance, exposing the remains of the murdered man. In life, he has some terrible enemies and their vengeance is not yet sated."

It was believed by family members that Henry Adams was responsible for blowing up Ira's grave and tombstone.

But there was no evidence and Henry was not charged in connection with any of these actions.

The Mullins family wasn't the first killing at Pound Gap. Thirty years earlier on March 16, 1862, the 42nd Ohio Infantry under the command of Brigadier General James. A. Garfield marched eight hundred Union solders through deep snow to engage Major John Thompson and his five hundred confederate troops. A deadly twenty minute battle ensued forcing the confederates to retreat from Pound Gap.

Brigadier General James A. Garfield later served as the 20th President of the United States being elected on March 4, 1881. His presidency lasted a mere two hundred days; he was shot by Charles J. Guiteau on July 2, 1881.

President Garfield was shot in the arm and back while waiting for the train to depart the Sixth Street Station of the Baltimore and Potomac Railroad. He finally succumbed to his wounds and died on September 18, 1881.

A short time before the Mullins massacre Doc Taylor was a feared hero for undertaking the dangerous mission of arresting the dreaded outlaw Talton Hall. Hall was reported to have killed nineteen men including the July 1891 cold blooded killing of Police Officer Enos Hylton.

On the day of the Hylton killing, Talton Hall and Miles Bates both were drinking heavily. Bates became very boisterous and Police Officer Enos Hylton approached the two men in a calm manner and asked them to be quiet. Bates starting cussing and Enos Hylton attempted to arrest him. Bates resisted arrest so Enos Hylton pulled his pistol on Bates.

Talton Hall, who had been standing quietly to one side, then drew his pistol and fired at Enos Hylton hitting him straight through the heart; he walked a few steps and fell to the ground dead.

The Dickenson County, Virginia Newspaper (Name Unknown) reports as follows:

"After his dastardly murder of Hylton, Hall fled the county and was not heard of again until late in the fall.

ARRESTED

He went to Memphis, TN and worked as a cab-driver. Here things went well with him until he was recognized at length as the man who was wanted at Wise Courthouse for the murder of Enos B. Hylton. He was immediately put under arrest and the authorities of Wise County were notified of this action. Parties at once went to Memphis and identified him, when he was turned over to the authorities and then brought to Gladesville. He was then incarcerated at the March term of the County court. He employed the best legal talent in Wise and adjoining counties.

It may be presumed that everything possible was done to secure his acquittal; but in spite of all legal efforts he was found guilty and sentenced to be hanged on the 4th day of June."

Talton Hall was apprehended in Memphis, Tennessee by three Knott County Deputies.

Doc Taylor and Sheriff Wilson Holbrook brought him back to Wise County for trial; Talton Hall was convicted and sent to Lynchburg Jail while his case was with the Court of Appeals.

One can only wonder if riding on the wave of a feared hero from the arrest of Talton Hall is what helped to make Doc Taylor's decision to take out his arch enemy Ira Mullins.

For her own protection, massacre witness Amanda Jane Mullins was held in the Wise County Jail for a six month period in protective custody for fear that the killers knew she had recognized them as they had communicated with her.

Several weeks would go by since the killings without a trace of the killers. Then, reports started to come in about Doc Taylor being on the back roads accompanied by several armed men.

One thing that Doc Taylor did during this time to keep the posse from tracking him was removing the heels from his boots and reattaching them to the toe.

This served to confuse anyone who would be tracking him by giving the impression he was traveling in the opposite direction.

On several occasions during the time of his evasion from the law, the attic loft of his son Sylvan and wife Hattie's home near Norton, Virginia served as one of his favorite hiding places.

At one point in July, Deputy Sheriff John Miller and his posse of twenty men caught up with several of the outlaws and had a gun battle in which Calvin and Henan Fleming were wounded.

The ALEXANDERIA VA, GAZETTE reported
the incident as follows:

ALEXANDERIA VA, GAZETTE

14 JUY 1893

"A dispatch from Norton, Wise County, says:
The Fleming gang has disappeared in the
mountains. Reliable parties have
communicated with relatives of the Flemings
and bring information that Henan Fleming
lies buried under a fallen tree, with only a few
leaves and brush to cover his body. His
brother Calvin is thought to be dead in a cave
nearby. Deputy Sheriff Miller and Marshall
Tom Osborne, of Norton, accompanied by
twenty men, returned yesterday morning
from the seat of war at Pound Gap. They
brought with them a Winchester rifle, a grip, a
bat, and a dog, which they captured from the
Fleming boys in the battle Monday morning.
They report both of the Flemings seriously, if
not fatally, wounded, but say they have made
their escape into Kentucky.

Ten of fifteen men are still in the mountains after them. Old Jefferson Fleming, the father of Cal [and] Henan (sic), is under guard at Glade Ville. The Flemings are wanted for the murder of the Mullins, which occurred in Pound Gap two years ago. The Flemings, in company with Doc Taylor, who is in jail in Lynchburg under sentence of death, killed the entire Mullins family of six with the exception of one little boy, who escaped into the mountains. They have defied the authorities for the past two years and caused a reign of terror to exist throughout that section. They also at one time belonged to the Talt Hall gang."

Calvin and Henan managed to get away; they first made their way to Elkhorn Creek and hid in a cave at Anderson's Branch. Calvin was shot in the chest and Henan was shot through the mouth knocking some of his teeth out. He was also shot in the shoulder.

A man named Sam Ratliff carried food to them during this recovery time. Because of the terrain, Sam couldn't get near the brothers; he had to use grapevines to swing the food across a cliff's ledge.

While in the cave recovering from their wounds, Calvin used a water drip from the roof of the cave to assist the healing process of his chest wound.

A short time later, after they recovered from the shoot-out, the Fleming brothers fled and laid low in West Virginia.

Methodist Minister Rev. Robin Wingfield Beverly, my 2nd great grandfather, was a preacher and mountain evangelist in the old Circuit Rider days. Circuit riding preachers would ride from town to town and hold tent and camp revivals. Living in Letcher Kentucky, they traveled a great deal in the parts of Virginia and Kentucky.

On one of these trips with his wife, Ardelia Dotson Beverly, a man came suddenly out of the woods and stopped them in their tracks near Pound Gap.

He jumped out like a wild tiger at them. Rev. Robin Beverly recognized him as Doc Taylor who had just weeks before been accused of murdering the Ira Mullins family at Pound Gap, and was now on the run evading the Law. Rev. Robin Beverly shared that he was a preacher headed for a camp revival and found favor with Doc Taylor to the point that Doc Taylor told them to go on their way.

But before they could leave, Doc Taylor asked Rev. Robin Beverly for a favor.

He thought that he was going to ask for his horse or some money but he only asked for his chewing tobacco. Thus, he gladly gave him all the tobacco he had. Doc Taylor told Rev. Robin Beverly and his wife to be certain they told no one about seeing him and then told them to proceed on their journey. Doc Taylor then disappeared back into the mountain woods as quickly as he appeared.

Alma Davis, my great Aunt, placed the following article in The Mountain People and Places Newspaper of Wise Virginia (date @1950's):

"Submitted by Alma Davis, Grandfather Beverly was a Methodist minister of the old "Circuit Rider" days. He traveled about a great deal in this part of Virginia and sometimes he had appointments in neighboring Kentucky. On one of these trips over Cumberland Mountain with mother, at Pound Cap, a man came out of the woods and stopped them.

Grandfather recognized him as Dr. M.B. Taylor, or who was better known especially as "Red Fox" in John Fox's Trail of the Lonesome Pine Taylor.

Sometime before, had murdered the Mullins family in the Gap of the mountain and was now dodging the law. He asked grandfather for tobacco, and he gave him all he had.

He told grandfather to be certain they told no one about seeing him and then told them to go on. Grandmother said they were very careful and scared until they got a long way from him."

Not long after this encounter, Doc Taylor boarded a train outfitted in new clothes that his son had purchased for him. He then entered an empty boxcar at Norton yard and rode the train into Bluefield, West Virginia.

Somehow word got to Wise County Commonwealth Attorney Robert Bruce and he wired the Baldwin Detective agency to apprehend Doc Taylor.

As soon as the train came to a stop, William G. Baldwin got the drop on Doc Taylor and already had his pistol pulled. William G. Baldwin and his Detectives arrested Doc Taylor without incident. They then returned the fugitive to Wise County for trial.

Part Three
The Trial of Hall and Taylor

In August 1892 the National Police Gazette Newspaper in New York described the story as follows:

"THE NATIONAL POLICE GAZETTE: NEW YORK

August 20, 1892

BRUTAL SOUTHERN BANDITS

They Are Cowardly Murderers and Hate Each Other.

Both in the Same Jail.

And They Are Anxious to Get at Each Other's Throat.

THE GALLOWS AWAITS THEM.

Two of the most notorious outlaws and murderers in Southwestern Virginia and Eastern Kentucky are Talton and "Doc" Taylor, the former soon to pay the penalty of his crimes with his life on the gallows and the other certain to follow him, after the legal formality of a trial.

These men, who would rank as bandit chiefs in Italy, are sworn and bitter enemies. Behind bars and wearing chains they met in Wise Court House, Va., on Thursday last. While at large in the border mountain their respective gangs had frequent conflicts with more or less fatal results, and it was settled that one or the other or both would die by each other's hands had not the law stepped in to save them the trouble. "Talt" Hall, as he is familiarly known, is the hero of no less than nineteen murders and was the most dreaded desperado in this section.

His latest victim was a policeman of Wise Court House, who, from a sense of duty, was rash enough to avow his determination to arrest the outlaw if he ever got the opportunity.

Hall heard of this and walked boldly into town and coolly and deliberately shot and killed the policeman in the streets and then fled. A liberal reward was offered and he was captured some months afterward in Memphis, Tenn. Hall had become so much of a terror that no one could be found to take the requisition papers and bring the outlaw back for trial.

It was at this juncture that Doc Taylor came to the front and offered to undertake the dangerous mission. His services were promptly accepted, and he not only brought his man back, but, amid great excitement, guarded him with a large posse in jail, and to and from court, during a trial that lasted over a week.

All this time Wise Court House was in a state of siege by Hall's follower's and outlaws from Kentucky, who threatened to rescue him. Taylor, however, headed a heavily armed body of citizens and by presenting a determined front defeated the purpose of Hall's sympathizers.

The latter was sentenced to be executed in June, and had to be taken to the jail at Lynchburg for safekeeping an appeal in his case had been. The Court of Appeals, the Wise County Court and when Hall was brought under a strong guard to. . .meantime and while. . .the Lynchburg jail, Doc Taylor, proud of his heroism in the Hall case, and with a certain safety from arrest, had full away over an already lawless border region. With a band of desperate followers he did almost anything he pleased.

His last cruel and inhuman crime, about six weeks ago, was the massacre of the Mullins family. Ira Mullins, his wife and two children and a driver were returning to Virginia in a wagon from Kentucky.

Mullins had nearly all his possessions with him, including some $400 in cash.

The families were set upon in the neighborhood of Pound Gap by Doc Taylor and his gang, and not one of them survived to tell the tale. Father, mother, children, and the driver were murdered, their bodies rifled and the wagon robbed of its contents.

The news of this crime spread rapidly, and the people of the entire country surrounding the scene became first alarmed and next united in a determination to hunt down Doc Taylor and his gang. Every man became a law officer, and after a pursuit which was close and marked by several skirmishes Taylor was finally captured and lodged in the Wise County Jail.

When Hall reached Wise Court House on Thursday afternoon last he learned for the first time that his old and deadly foe, Taylor was a prisoner, and, like himself, an inmate of the same jail.

This aroused all the hatred in the outlaw's nature, and he fairly writhed in his manacles with the desire for vengeance.

He asked to be allowed to see Taylor, but the guards refused. Hall's eye's flashed and he swore he would see him, but the prison authorities were obstinate and denied his request, though he promised not to make any violent demonstration.

At length the Commonwealth's Attorney, Bruce, directed that Hall should be allowed to stop at the door of Taylor's cell for a few moments. When he was taken there, Taylor, anxious to make friendly overtures, thrust his hand through the bars of his cell to shake hands. Hall instantly flew into a rage and struck Taylor through the bars with his heavily manacled hand.

He cursed him, his face livid and white, and his eyes glowed in the dim light of the corridor as he shook his finger in Taylor's face and hissed through his clenched teeth, "Do you reckon I'd shake hands, with you. I never shot a man in the back.

I never shot a dead man's eyes out and then put him up as you did Ira Mullins.

I never killed women and children. You had better be down on your knees praying to God for mercy.

Hall was forced back to his cell. Taylor was apparently unmoved by this torrent of abuse. "Take him away, boys," was all he said. The guards willingly did so, for it was no pleasant feeling to be witnesses to such a scene between two such men, although they were manacled and separated. Hall will be hanged on Sept. 2."

The Washington Post in September 1892 described the situation as follows:

"THE WASHINGTON POST

Friday, September 2, 1892

TALTON HALL IN HIGH GLEE

The Desperado Facing His Doom in Drunken Hilarity

HE PINES FOR VENGEANCE

The Mountain Murderer Exhorts His Sister to Put Out of the Way Three Persons Whom He Promises to Name on the Scaffold-- Precautions Taken Against an Attempt to Rescue Him by His Friends--Record of a Life Spent in Crime.

Norton Va., Sept. 1-[Special]:-This is the last night on earth for Talton Hall, the Kentucky desperado and murderer of so many men and he is preparing to shuffle off in gleeful manner, as liquor is constantly pouring down his throat. For two days he has been more or less under its influence, and most any visitor to his call is permitted to give him a drink.

It is predicted by many that he will cheat the gallows by committing suicide tonight. His sister, Mrs. Bates, was in conference with him for a long time this afternoon, and gave him some tea. What it might have contained there is no telling. The conversation with his sister was long and earnest. He told her there were three men whom she must put out of the way if she had to sell the cattle on every hill and all the feathers in the tick. He refused to give her the names, anything he would do go tomorrow on the scaffold. It is thought he has reference to Judge Skeen, who sentenced him, and Private Detective Bride and "Doc" Taylor, who is now confined in jail for the killing of Moonshiner Ira Mullins and family at Pound Gap.

It will be remembered that Taylor is his bitter enemy. He is the father of the murdered Hylton's brother-in-law, and busied himself in Hall's capture.

Last night Hall applied the blaze from his lamp to the bed clothes and would have burned the jail but for the timely arrival of the guard.

He made the attempt twice. When questioned as to his reason, he laughingly replied that he wanted to smoke "Doc" Taylor out of the adjoining cell. Two reporters called at the cell late this evening. He was dressed elegantly in a neat-fitting suit of black.

His conversation flowed fluently, and was witty. "You see," he said, "in order to keep up my spirits I have to keep the spirits down," and he asked for another drink, which was given him.

Hall informed the reporters that he was certain to go to Heaven. F. J. Luckle, the Catholic priest of Lynchburg, is expected here and will remain with Hall, who is a member of his church.

The gallows was constructed in a small barracks, which will hold fifty people, to be composed of medical men, preachers, newspaper men, guards, and the sheriff and jailer. People are now pouring in and by 10 o'clock to-morrow there will be 5,000 people, who will only be allowed to see the corpse.

There are no fears of an attempted rescue, though the 100 soldiers are vigilant.

The hanging will occur between 10 and 2 o'clock. Talton Hall's criminal record has probably never been paralleled in the United States. He is credited with ninety-nine murders, and while this is probably an exaggeration there is no doubt that he is responsible for the death of at least two-score men.

He was born in Letcher County, Ky., forty-six years ago and grew up with such desperadoes as John Wright, who is credited with twenty-seven murders, and the "Doc" Taylor against whom he is now so bitter.

These men joined Morgan's band when the war broke out, and made themselves conspicuous for their deeds of reckless daring.

When the war ended they returned to Kentucky and inaugurated a reign of terror in the mountains.

Murders were the daily amusement of the gang, and although they were frequently arrested the terror which they inspired insured their acquittal when brought to trial. He began his career of crime at a very early age.

When he was thirteen years of age his brothers, John S. and Marshall were killed by George Hank.

They were Confederate soldiers, and Hank commanded a bushwhacking company known as the 10th Kentucky Mounted Infantry. Talt's brothers were returning to the army from a furlough, when Hank took them prisoners for purposes of robbery and revenge and then killed them. Talt swore revenge, and started off by killing his brother's assassins.

He was in all the battles of the Howards, Turners, and Eversoles, and had several vendettas of his own.

It was well known that any juror who voted to convict any of the desperadoes would be marked by their friends.

And as a consequence they always escaped. In this way Hall was acquitted of the cold-blooded murder of Henry Maggard in 1866. He killed Dan Pridmore in 1875 and was acquitted.

A cowardly jury acquitted him of Nat Baker's murder in 1881, and he went free when he murdered his brother-in-law, Henry Triplett, in 1882. He killed Henry Houk in 1883, and was indicted but no officer dared arrest him. and in 1885 he killed his cousin, Mack Hall, and laughed at the sheriff who tried to arrest him. Finally, on July 14, 1891, he deliberately murdered Chief of Police Hylton of Norton, Virginia. By this time public sentiment was too strong for him and he fled the country.

He was captured at Memphis, Tenn., however and brought back for trial. He was duly tried and convicted. An appeal to the Supreme Court resulted in an affirmation of the sentence, and the governor refused to commute it. The result is that tomorrow he will at last face the fate he so often meted out to others."

Great and many rumors were spread that Talton Hall's clan including "Devil" John Wright would try to rescue him from the gallows. For two full days and nights, a band of the friends of Talton Hall (about seventy five men all from over the Kentucky line) lay in the woods in the vicinity of the town. They were awaiting an opportunity to sweep down upon the jail and courthouse.

A spy was sent into town but he was arrested. The strong preparations and show of force made for the gang's reception frightened them off with most of the men returning back to their homes.

On the outskirts of town and along all the roads, Sheriff Deputies and appointed law men were stopping and disarming every man who was carrying a weapon.

Guards were placed around the clock at every road and every path leading into town, within a radius of one-half mile from the Wise County Courthouse.

The guards drilled twice each day in the fields around the courthouse. Over one hundred law officers joined the security detail.

On the day of Talton Hall's hanging, a large crowd had gathered hoping to hear Hall confess. Yet, Talton Hall would not admit to any of his crimes even though his lawyers and his priest, Father Lockie, wanted him to confess. He came to the window, his lips opened and closed but no one heard a sound.

His sister brought him a white handkerchief to tie around his throat once his body was cut down to conceal the red mark of the rope.

In iron shackles, Hall bid them a final farewell. Then, without any emotion, he stepped out with a firm step. A black cap was then drawn over his features, the rope adjusted to firmly fit his neck. Two upright beams had to be knocked from under the trap door causing more suspense with each blow. Finally, the Sheriff cried in a loud voice, "May God have mercy on this poor man's soul." The rope was subsequently cut and Talton Hall was hung to death.

After a few muscular twitches his body hung limp and after hanging for seventeen minutes he was pronounced dead by the attending physicians.

Family and friends took his body back to John Wright's home with over one hundred people following the body. To ensure that Talton Hall's remains would not be disturbed, they buried him in an unmarked grave.

During the time of his death, a young boy named Uriah N. Webb wrote a poem about Old Talt Hall. It goes as follows:

Come all you fathers and mothers,

Brothers and sister all.

I'll relate to you a story,

The story of old Talt Hall.

He's breaking up our country

And trying to kill us all.

He shot and killed Frank Slayers,

Was the commencement of it all.

He left his ol' Kentucky

Virginia for to roam,

Leaving his friends and loved ones

Back in his Beaver Creek home.

He roamed the streets of Wise and Norton

Through the summer and the fall.

He met with Enos Hylton,

And poor Enos had to fall.

The posse hunted for him

Through valley, hill, and dale.

They found him down in Memphis,

And he had to go to jail.

They arrested him in Tennessee.

They brought him to Gladeville jail,

Without any friends or relations,

No one to go his bail.

They built the platform, boys,

Nearby the jailhouse side.

He walked out on it and wrung his hands and cried,

If I hadn't killed Enos Hylton, I wouldn't have to die.

Once the Baldwin Detectives brought Doc Taylor to Wise County, he was indicted, tried, and convicted of the crime of murder.

Once again, Sheriff Deputies and appointed law men were stopping and disarming every man who was carrying a weapon.

Guards were placed around the clock at every road and every path leading into town, within a radius of one-half mile from the Wise County Courthouse.

The Courthouse was two stories tall and had four cells; two were on the upper level and two were on the main level. Guards set up barricades and cut portholes through the walls which were used as gun-ports. The presiding judge was the Honorable Samuel W. Williams of Wytheville Virginia. The commonwealth attorney was Robert Bruce. Doc Taylor's counsel was T.M. Alderson and William Miller.

The grand jury consisted of the foreman J.M. Wampler, Robert J. Beverly, Ellis Dean, William Roberson, H.P. Carter and James Youell. They returned the indictment for the murder to wit:

"The jurors of the grand jury of the Commonwealth of Virginia, empaneled, charged and sworn in and for the body of Wise County, at a term of the county court of said county, commencing on Tuesday, the 26th day of July, 1892, and now attending said court, upon their oath present that M. B. Taylor on the _ day of May, 1892, with force and arms in the county aforesaid, in and upon the body of one Ira Mullins, in the peace of said Commonwealth, then and there being feloniously, willfully, and of his malice aforethought, did make an assault, and that the said M. B. Taylor, a certain gun, of the value of five dollars, then and there charged with gunpowder and one leaden bullet, which said gun, he, the said M. B. Taylor, in his hands then and there had and held, then and there feloniously, willfully, and of his malice aforethought.

Did discharge and shoot off, to, against, and upon the said Ira Mullins and that the said M. B. Taylor, discharged and shot off as aforesaid, then and there feloniously, willfully, and of his malice aforethought, did strike, penetrate and wound the said Ira Mullins in and upon the face, head, shoulders, thighs and chin of him, the said Ira Mullins, giving to him the said Ira Mullins, then and there with the leaden bullets aforesaid, so as aforesaid discharged and shot out of the gun aforesaid, by the said M. B. Taylor, in and upon the face, head, shoulders, thighs and chin of him, the said Ira Mullins five mortal wounds, of which said mortal wounds he, the said Ira Mullins then and there instantly died.

And so the jurors aforesaid upon their oaths aforesaid, do say that the said M. B. Taylor, him, the said Ira Mullins, in the manner and by the means aforesaid, feloniously, willfully, and of his malice aforethought, did kill and murder, against the peace and dignity of the Commonwealth."

The Second Count addressed the certain pistol of Doc Taylor and was witnessed by Amanda Jane Mullins, the sister of Ira Mullins and the wife of Wilson Mullins.

Doc Taylor's attorneys entered a plea of not guilty to the indictment.

Jurors Joel Beverly, John Hughs, Alex Trent, William Wolfe, James H. Elkins, G. F. Jones, George C. Skeens, D. F. Wells, F. P. Graham, John B. Willis, Palsur Debusk, I. N. Mills, James M. Hillman, Samuel May, M. T. Evans, and Elisha Tate were qualified, the counsel for Doc Taylor struck four of the jurymen that had been selected namely, John B. Willis, George C. Skeen, G. F. Jones, and James M. Hillman.

Evidence at the scene showed the killers used a Winchester rifle that shot rim fired 45.75 caliber shells. More evidence introduced in the trial concerning his Winchester rifle showed that Doc Taylor's rifle used center-fired shells. But Deputy Sheriff John Miller testified, and after close scrutiny, the court saw that the plunger on Doc Taylor's rifle had been cleverly tampered with by someone.

The firing pin was altered to strike the center of a cartridge instead of on the rim of the shell.

This crucial fact proved that someone had tampered with the firing pin in attempts to benefit Doc Taylor.

During the trial, Reuben McFall testified that Doc Taylor proposed to him at various times to assist him in killing the Mullins Boys (Ira and his brother, Henderson), and if he would not go with him, he would be damned if he would not go by himself.

Granville Cox testified that Taylor tried several times to get him to go to Kentucky with him to kill Ira Mullins and Henderson Mullins and if I don't get it done this year, I will do it next year or have it done.

At one point during the search for the killers, the posse received word of their hide out. Booker Mullins testified he was one of the guards with Deputy McFall that went to arrest Doc Taylor and the Flemings.

And while going down the hill, his foot slipped and the cap was burst on his gun (which was cocked).

He claimed that Doc Taylor and the Flemings then started firing at them.

Miss May Brauham and Logan Notthingham testified that they saw Doc Taylor and Calvin Fleming, on Sunday night before the killing, going in the direction of Pound gap, riding fast, and sitting up straight in their saddles.

After six days of trial on Saturday, September 10, 1892, the deliberating jury returned the following verdict;

"We the jury, find the prisoner, M. B. Taylor, guilty of murder of the first degree. (Signed) Wm. Wolfe, Foreman."

Upon his conviction, Doc Taylor at once moved the court in arrest of judgment and to set aside the verdict of the jury and grant him a new trial for various grounds of error assigned at bar. The court at once overruled this motion.

On July 6, 1893, the Supreme Court of Wytheville refused to grant a new trial and affirmed the judgment of the lower Wise County court. Doc Taylor was returned from the Lynchburg jail to the Wise County jail.

Upon his return, the deputy clerk informed him that he had been tried by an impartial jury of his county, had been represented by able counsel, and had been found guilty of murder of the first degree.

In addition, he was informed that his case had been appealed to the supreme court of the state, and that the court, after reviewing his case, had affirmed the judgment of the lower court.

The deputy clerk asked Doc Taylor if he had anything to say about why the court should not proceed to pass final judgement upon him and re-fix the day of his hanging.

Doc Taylor replied "I have not, but a friend, a witness, will speak for me." Judge Morrison asked, "Who is your witness?" Doc Taylor answered: "The Lord Jesus Christ. Will you hear Him?" Judge Morrison answered: "I will."

Doc Taylor read from this Leather pocket Bible several chapters from Psalms dealing with false witnesses and oppression. After a few minutes, Judge Morrison stopped him and stated: "Dr. Taylor, I fear you have invoked the sacred name of Jesus Christ for a selfish and improper purpose. If you have done that, I would commend you to approach Him aright with a humble and contrite spirit, realizing you are a sinner and have great need of His aid and assistance, and when you do that, regardless of what have been your sins and short-comings in the past, we are told you will get complete forgiveness and there will come to you a sense of forgiveness and sweet communion that will fortify and sustain you through the great ordeal through which you are about to pass. I beseech you to seek this course of forgiveness and to prepare to meet your God."

Then Judge Morrison re-set the day of his hanging for October 27, 1893 between 10a.m. and 4p.m.

An accomplice indictment was also brought against Calvin and Henan Fleming's father Robert Jefferson Fleming.

But when the trial was called the witness was absent. No evidence was found against Robert Jefferson Fleming and the indictment was dropped. Robert Jefferson Fleming died during the trial period of Doc Taylor in August 1893 in Virginia.

Doc Taylor claimed to be a special ward of heaven, he also threatened dire vengeance upon all who participated in his execution and lynching. He requested to preach his own funeral sermon and it was granted. Like Jesus, Doc Taylor also stated he too would rise again after three days. He claimed to be a "Seer", one who had the ability to communicate with spirits and angels.

Before his death, some of his friends claimed he had become insane and circulated a petition to ask the Governor to commute his sentence to life in prison. Only a hand full of people signed the petition.

The day before his execution he was led from the jail cell and he stood at the jail window with a little table beside him. The sky was overcast and a light rain was falling. A large crowd with a small sea of umbrellas had gathered in the rain to hear him.

An old woman in black with a black sunbonnet drawn close to her face was beside him. She had made him a white outfit and a white cap to cover his head. On the table beside them, a few pieces of bread were placed for his last communion. He administered the communion to himself. He then lifted the bread and asked the rain soaked crowd to come forward and partake with him in the last sacrament.

None in the crowd moved but the old woman who was believed to be his wife turned her face toward him. Doc Taylor pushed the bread over to the old woman and she took the bread.

The rest of the sermon was full of un-forgiveness, and rambling; just like Hall, he too never once admitted any guilt or sin.

The next day he appeared again in his white suit and walked to the scaffold steps.

Some of the people in the crowd were weeping, some were silently worshiping. But all came to see the hanging. Doc Taylor's upper body was visible above the scaffold box. He had his hands tied behind his back with a white handkerchief; he started voicing passages of scripture and praying in a low and soft voice.

After a short time, jailor Charles Hughes slipped the white cap that the old lady had made for him over his head, and he then slipped the noose over his head and adjusted the rope accordingly to his neck. At that moment, jailor Jeff Hunsucker jolted the trap door causing Doc Taylor to crumple to the floor. A few seconds went by and then he straightened back up to the standing position.

The Sheriff gave the order to cut the trap door rope and Doc Taylor dropped to the end of his rope. He started twisting and would unwind and he struggled, whirling for some time.

When the twisting of the rope stopped, Dr. Miles and Dr. Cherry pronounced him dead after hanging by his neck for nineteen minutes.

After he was pronounced dead, Doc Taylor's body was then delivered to family members; the body was kept up for three days as this was his request. He did not rise on the third day as he had stated he would do and the body was interred on a hill side near his home where it lies to this day.

John Wesley Powers, a Wise County Sheriff's jailers that were present and working security at the time of both hangings stated that hundreds of people came from all around to see the hangings like an attraction.

PART FOUR
THE ARREST OF THE FLEMINGS

Big Ed Hall (who was known as "The Mountain Man Hunter") was hunting down the Fleming brothers.

Roughly just over a year had passed following the murder of Ira Mullins. Thus, the $700 reward was still being offered by the Wise County authorities. The rumor mill was quite active with the notion that the Fleming brothers had fled to West Virginia. The Law men received word that the brothers had become braggarts about their role in the killings.

Authorities were still searching for the Fleming brothers. Additional men including Big Ed Hall, were Gooseneck John H. Branham, Albert John Wesley, and A. J. Swindall.

In January 1894, during their investigation they paid for some letters and seized a number of letters from family members in Wise County, Virginia.

Fortunately, information was obtained from these letters that suggested the Fleming brothers might be working at a saw mill logging operation under assumed names in the vicinity of Boggs, Webster County, West Virginia.

On Friday morning January 5, 1894, Big Ed Hall and his posse gathered together and took the train from Norton, Virginia over to Bluefield, West Virginia. The men walked and camped in the mountain woods for days along this route.

Just a few hours prior to sundown on one particular day, the group reached the edge of the town of Boggs and set up camp. Big Ed Hall deployed a scout who determined that the Fleming brothers indeed were working at the mill. The scout also learned as well that the brothers typically travelled into town on weekend days to check for mail at the Post Office, which also served as the General Store.

This discovery of collecting their mail led to the undoing of the Fleming brothers the very next day on January 14, 1894.

The group of righteous men set positions at several locations around the post office and were ready to attack the killers.

It was so cold that some of the men stood watch in a dwelling house about fifty yards away. Before long, A. J. Swindall caught sight of the two men while approaching the Post Office on horseback and he turned to Big Ed Hall and John H. Branham, stating, "I see them coming."

The Law men were very eager to pounce as they observed the Fleming brothers enter the Post Office. Knowing that the Fleming brothers had no regard for Law enforcement officers from several previous shoot outs, and the unprovoked killing of the Mullins family, they both had allegedly confessed their guilt and said that their arrest meant the worst to them.

They had let it be known that they would rather die rather than submit to being arrested; the posse's stress level was extremely high! As a result, they immediately sprinted to the door as soon as it had closed.

These Law men had all drawn their pistols and were ready to fire. They swiftly opened the door and stepped into the Post Office. Henan Fleming was adjacent to Calvin Fleming who was standing near the window while getting ready to open a letter.

The innocent bystanders were of noticeable concern with the post office being a very small location.

It was filled with approximately thirteen additional people aside from the posse and the two killers. This post office was a mere 252 square feet in size. Nonetheless, the Law men yelled as loudly as possible for the Fleming brothers to drop their weapons and surrender to the authorities at once.

Although caught by surprise and disorderly, the Flemings simply refused to comply with the direct order. The criminals instead headed to the back of the building while pulling their pistols. In the same moment, many of the frantic residents rushed the door hoping to leave but ended up in the middle between the Law men and the killers.

Only seconds passed before both groups began firing; Big Ed Hall was the first to be shot but fortunately was only grazed to the head and fell down momentarily. Nevertheless, he was able to pull himself back up from the floor and fired a point blank range shot that killed Calvin Fleming instantly.

A.J. Swindall was seriously wounded suffering from a neck shot as John H. Branham lay seriously wounded on the floor beside him after being shot. John H. Branham was still able to shoot Henan Fleming.

Henan Fleming had been shot in the back and arm, and was bleeding tremendously. The arm shot hit the cylinder of his pistol first, split in half, cutting his hand all the way up to his elbow.

As Henan turned his head, he soon discovered the pistol of Big Ed Hall was pointed in his face. Big Ed Hall yelled, "Blast you, Henan, you have killed my men. Give up or I'll finish you! I'll kill you like I killed Calvin." A.J. Swindall was still bleeding profusely from his neck and mouth.

He walked outside by the creek and splashed some ice cold water on his wounds.

Consequently, his actions stopped the bleeding and in turn most likely saved his life.

He later stated, "I thought I was a gone sucker for a moment."

Calvin Fleming was buried by his logging coworkers at the Boggs cemetery off of Wildcat / Barnett Run Road, not too far from the place where he was killed.

John H. Branham died nine days later from his wounds and was laid to rest at the very same cemetery as Calvin Fleming. John's wife Nancy was pregnant at the time of his murder, but the child died at birth.

We will never know how much the stress of these unfortunate circumstances may have contributed to the death of this child.

Big Ed Hall, A.J. Swindall, and Albert John Wesley, all remained in Boggs with John H. Branham until his death and burial. They then went to Camden, through Bluefield and then back home.

The letter that Calvin Fleming was about to open just before he was shot was obtained and read by one of the Law men.

This letter had been sent from Jervey Caudill, a Wise County, Virginia resident.

The letter simply stated, "Look out, John Branham, Doc Swindall, and Ed Hall are after you."

Jervey Caudill likely mailed his letter around the same time that the posse left Wise County and was heading to the town of Boggs. It is ironic that in the time it took the letter to arrive, Big Ed Hall and his posse could have hand delivered it to Calvin and Henan Fleming.

While recovering from his wounds and before his court date, Henan Fleming confessed to his part in the murder of the Mullins family during questioning.

He went on trial July 24, 1894, and the Commonwealth Attorney attempted for six days to show that Henan Fleming was indeed one of the killers. But the main witness, Amanda Jane Mullins, was not in court to testify against him.

For reasons unknown Amanda was a no show at the trial. Some say Amanda was murdered. They say she married Isaac Belcher on November 23rd 1892 after the murder of her husband and was shot and killed on February 15th, 1894 by Orbin "Orb" Fleming, the younger brother to Henan and Calvin Fleming.

The Roanoke Times Newspaper reported the following:

The Roanoke Times, February 16, 1894 WAS A FLEMMING THE ASSASSIN? Reported Murder of the Widow Mullins by "Orb" Fleming

"CLINTWOOD, VA., Feb. 15 - The TIMES correspondent has just learned that "Orb" Fleming, a brother to the outlaws, Cal and Henan, shot and killed a woman in the vicinity of Pound Gap, where the Mullins family was murdered in the spring of 1892. This woman was the widow of Wilson Mullins, one of the murdered parties of that family. The report says that she was about the premises of her home, and was shot by someone secreted in the brush some distance from the house, and circumstances point to Fleming as the perpetrator of the foul crime. The theory of the motive is that, as Mrs. Mullins was the material witness against Henan Fleming, she was killed to destroy evidence against him.

Young Fleming is a desperate character and is following the footsteps of his brothers, despite their terrible fate, and his course will inevitably bring him to the same end. He is not more than twenty years of age. "

Some say she died in child birth on February 15th, 1894. There is an Amanda Belcher buried in Murdered Man's Cemetery with this date of death.

It is certainly understandable, with all Amanda had been through keeping her locked up for six months in protective custody before the first trial, that she would be "no show" at the second trial. We can speculate on the matter somewhat, but cannot state with certainty at this time the reasons as to the lack of her appearance that day in history. I would imagine that personal death threats may have been the culprit as you will soon see, murder was still afoot. And from the above newspaper article it is possible to Orbin Fleming did murder Amanda to save his brother Henan from hanging.

The Commonwealth Attorney could not get Henan Fleming on the stand and also could not use his confession against him. The Wise County Court was thereby forced to free Henan of all charges and dismissed the case. He lived the rest of his life out in Webster and Nicholas County, West Virginia as a night watchman for a railroad company and a police officer in Richwood. Henan died of natural causes on November 18th, 1943. He is buried in the Fleming Cemetery in Cottle, Nicholas County West Virginia.

Orbin Fleming moved with Henan to West Virginia and died on May 2nd, 1950 in Camden on Gauley in Webster County. He is also buried in the Fleming Cemetery in Cottle, Nicholas County West Virginia.

The follow year, Nancy Branham, John's widow married Deputy Sheriff William Renfro. William later became Chief of Police in Dorchester Virginia.

In yet another tragic turn of events for Nancy her second husband William Renfro was murdered on June 17, 1906 by an unknown assailant while investigating shots fired near the suburbs of the town.

The Reading Eagle Newspaper reported the incident on June 18, 1906 as follows:

CHIEF OF POLICE KILLED

"Roanoke, Va., June 18, -Chief of Police William Renfro, of Dorchester, Va., was shot and killed at that place last night by unknown parties. Renfro heard shooting in the suburbs of the town and started to investigate it, when he was fired upon, two shots taking effect and causing his death at an early hour this morning.

The officer made a dying statement, saying that he did not recognize his assailants and so far there is no clue to their identity.

Renfro had been Chief of Police of Dorchester, which is a mining town, for a number of years, and was held in high esteem."

PART FIVE
THE FINAL SHOTS

On a cold winter's day on January 31, 1895, (only a little more than a year after the Boggs town shoot out), Big Ed Hall was shot as he was gathering firewood near his shed. An unknown person fired a rifle from the second story window of the Martin Soward's store across from Big Ed Hall's home.

The bullet struck Big Ed Hall directly in the back. He ran and grabbed his Winchester rifle from the corner of the shed and then bolted to the front porch of his neighbor where he collapsed and died. Witnesses, including Hall's wife saw smoke coming from the second story window of the store.

No one actually saw the rifle or the shooter, the witnesses only saw the smoke. Some in the community would say that Arch Hopkins or Melvin Robinson possibly could have fired the shot since they were in the store at the time of the shooting.

However, a witness named Isaac Cantrell came forward and said he would take an oath on the Bible that both men were standing on the porch on the main floor when the shot was fired from upstairs. Thus, no one was charged and the murder was never solved.

Some family members believe that Calvin, Henan and Orbin's sister Ferbia Roxie (Fleming) Addington fired the shot from the upstairs window that killed Ed Hall. They also believe she made the green veils that partially covered the upper part of Doc Taylor and the Fleming brother's faces during the Pound Gap Massacre.

Her family also followed Henan to West Virginia. She died on March 31st, 1947. She is buried in Blacks Chapel Cemetery, in Camden on Gauley, Webster County, West Virginia.

The last murder charge on the court docket was against Henry Adams for his possible involvement with the Ira Mullins party murders. These charges against Henry Adams remained on the court docket until 1901 and were finally dismissed for insufficient evidence.

About the same time they dismissed his murder charges for insufficient evidence, Henry Adams was in prison for killing a son (John Phillip Wright) of "Devil" John Wright. He spent prison time from January 1899 until he was pardoned on May 8th, 1901. Henry was married to Eliza Jane (Mullins) Adams but he was after the wife of John Phillip Wright.

On September 12th, 1898, John Phillip Wright and Henry got into an argument over John's wife while drinking at a local whiskey house. Henry left the house first and John went after him. John saw Henry hide behind a tree and dismounted his horse. Henry shot John while he was standing behind the neck of his horse. He walked up to John and shot him several more times killing him.

John Phillip Wright was known for shooting "Bad" Frank Phillips through the hip. This shooting is told to have occurred in September of 1895. "Bad" Frank Phillips was a hired gun used by the McCoy family to retaliate against the Hatfields.

During the Ira Mullins killing trial, Reuben McFall and Granville Cox both testified that Doc Taylor wanted Henderson Mullins killed. It is believed that Doc Taylor made the deal Henry Adams to kill Henderson before he was hung.

Later, this same year, indeed the deal was done, Ira Mullins's brother Henderson Mullins was murdered on October 15, 1901.

The story is told that just about five months after his release from prison, Henry Adams killed Henderson Mullins over an argument involving a pet dog. Mullins family members believe that Henry Adams murdered Henderson over a deal made with Doc Taylor before Doc Taylor was hung.

On July 11th, 1905, Henry Adams was shot and arrested by Deputy Marshall Albritton Potter in Elkhorn Creek. This shoot-out lasted over fifteen minutes. Henry was operating his moonshine still when he was raided by a posse of Deputy Marshalls.

Henry Adams lived the rest of his life dodging and hiding from "Devil" John Wight for the murder of his son, John Phillip Wright. Henry died of natural causes on February 12, 1935.

On a particular interesting note, the last person hung in Wise County Virginia was Clifton Branham, he was the man that went to prison for killing Henry Vanover and claimed, "I got some money for the killing, but I did not kill Henry Vanover."

Not long after being paroled for killing Henry Vanover, Clifton moved back to the Wise County area but did not live with his wife Nancy. On December 22, 1902 during a family squabble Clifton shot and killed his wife Nancy on the dirt road near their home.

Clifton quickly fled to Kentucky and married his first cousin, in January 1903; a posse was dispatched to apprehend him. Emmett Swindall and John Wesley Hillman brought Clifton back to the Wise County jail to await indictment and trial.

Court convened on 28 January 1903 and endorsed the following indictment: Commonwealth of Virginia vs. Clifton Branham, Indictment for Murder.

The jury found Clifton Branham guilty of killing his wife, Nancy Branham, and ordered him hung by the neck until dead. The execution was set for Friday, September 25, 1903. Clifton Braham was hanged on the appointed day.

The End.

Over the years, many strange happenings have occurred at the Pound Gap. The latest strange happening occurred in 1998, during construction of a section of Highway US 23, the Pound Gap Thrust Fault was exposed.

Hmm, the Pound Gap Thrust Fault? There are also websites that share stories about hauntings at the Killing Rock at Pound Gap.

The collision of the North American Continent with Africa and Europe more than 275 million years ago formed the Appalachian Mountains. Geologists consider this exposed rock to be one of the most remarkable exposures of rock in the entire eastern United States.

The Kentucky Society of Professional Geologists declared on September 26, 1998, the Pound Gap, as Kentucky's first Distinguished Geologic Site.

The Letcher County Tourism and Convention Commission sponsors a nature hike along the Red Fox Trail (AKA Doc Taylor) that is marked with historical markers. You will walk the same wagon road and visit the site where the Massacre occurred in 1892.

After the hike, you can visit the Potter Cemetery at Forest Hill in Jenkins which is now well known as the Murdered Man Cemetery. It is reported to have twenty two murdered victims buried there.

This cemetery is on top of a mountain overlooking Jenkins and is located on the Mayo Trail highway near the Camden section of Jenkins.

My family is related to the Mullins, Fleming, Beverly, Dotson, Powers, Baldwin, Bolling, Estep, Caudill, Cantrell, Rose, Renfro, and Roberts's families in this story. Maybe several others!

SOURCES

The Courier Journal of Louisville Kentucky July 25, 1885.

Richmond Dispatch of Clintwood, Virginia August 15, 1892.

The Mountain People and Places Newspaper of Wise Virginia Submitted by Alma Davis @ 1950.

The National Police Gazette, New York August 20, 1892.

The Washington Post, September 2, 1892.

Poem Old Talt Hall by Uriah N. Webb.

Wise County Court documents and witness statements.

The Dickenson County Virginia Newspaper (Name Unknown) 1892.

Ancestry.com Records on family members.

The Reading Eagle Newspaper Roanoke Virginia June 18, 1906.

The Southeastern Reporter, Volume 17, Virginia.

Wikipedia, the free encyclopedia – Pound Gap.

The Roanoke Times Newspaper, February 16, 1894.

ACKNOWLEDGEMENTS

I would like to extend a special thank you to my wife Doris Gail Barber Baldwin, whose love and giving support make all things possible. A true Proverbs 31: 10-31 wife.

To my son Roy Dean Baldwin, many thanks for your long hours and hard work.

To my daughter Amanda Baldwin, many thanks for your long hours and hard work.

To my friend Daniel Quinn Woolard for your hard work and dedication.

Check out my other stories and books at:

http://thebaldwinstories.wix.com/author-blog

Facebook page:

https://www.facebook.com/TheBaldwinStories

Please remember to write a review on Amazon.

Contact email: thebaldwinstories@gmail.com

To Molly,
Enjoy Reading!
Doris Baldwin

Oakly Dean Baldwin

Made in the USA
Coppell, TX
28 January 2022

72471978R00056